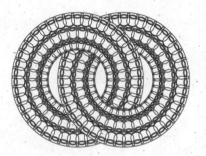

Eleanor

Eleanor

Gray Jacobik

CAVANKERRY PRESS

CavanKerry Press Ltd.
Fort Lee, New Jersey
www.cavankerrypress.org

Publisher's Cataloging-In-Publication Data
(Prepared by The Donohue Group, Inc.)
Names: Jacobik, Gray, author.
Title: Eleanor / Gray Jacobik.
Description: First edition. | Fort Lee, New Jersey : CavanKerry Press, 2020. | Includes
   bibliographical references.
Identifiers: ISBN 9781933880754
Subjects: LCSH: Roosevelt, Eleanor, 1884–1962—Family—Poetry. | Roosevelt, Eleanor,
   1884–1962—Friends and associates—Poetry. | Roosevelt, Eleanor, 1884–1962—Political
   and social views—Poetry. | Presidents' spouses—United States—Poetry. | LCGFT:
   Biographical poetry.
Classification: LCC PS3560.A249 E44 2020 | DDC 811/.54—dc23

Cover and interior text design by Mayfly Design
First Edition 2020, Printed in the United States of America

CavanKerry Press is grateful for the support it receives from the New Jersey State Council on the Arts.

Also by Gray Jacobik

Jane's Song (1976)
Paradise Poems (1978)
Sandpainting (1980)
The Double Task (1998)
The Surface of Last Scattering (1999)
Brave Disguises (2002)
Little Boy Blue: A Memoir in Verse (2011)
The Banquet: New & Selected Poems (2016)

For Christianne Mason Garofalo
and all courageous women who lead

*When will our consciences grow so tender
that we will act to prevent human misery
rather than avenge it?*

—Eleanor Roosevelt

*No woman has ever so comforted the
distressed—or distressed the comfortable.*

—Clare Boothe Luce

Contents

Marriage & Family

Betrayal

Aftermath

Friends & Lovers

A Politician's Wife / First Lady

After the White House

Epilogue

Prologue

1

I was born Anna Eleanor Roosevelt
called Eleanor after my father, Elliott.

My daughter is Anna Eleanor, called
Anna. Her daughter, my granddaughter,

bears our name as well, only we call
her Sistie. Anna Eleanor Roosevelt

is the name I bore until I married
Franklin and added a second field

of roses, from the Dutch, to my name.
Soon I will be name only: Anna

Eleanor Roosevelt Roosevelt: Anna
after my mother who died at twenty-nine,

Eleanor after my father who died
at thirty-four, field of roses, field

of roses. A name to be carved in stone—
yet a vision if you will see it—one

field of roses followed by another . . .

Substitutes
& Servants

2

The first servant I remember
was my nurse, Madeleine,
who taught me to read

and to sew. She scolded
in unkind, even cruel ways.
If I darned my socks

imperfectly, she would cut
enormous holes in them.
Blind with tears, sulking,

my pinpricked fingers
bloodied, I would darn
for hours until I heard

Parfait Mademoiselle!
and I could flee her severe
domain. So easily humiliated,

I never said a word until,
almost fourteen, I confided
to Grandmama, who fired

Madeleine that very hour.

3

circa 1891–1897

Our laundress at Tivoli was quite Madeleine's
      opposite. An immigrant from Bohemia,

large, cheerful, robust: I adored the hours I spent
      with her in the steamy laundry or sunny

courtyard. I'd prattle on with complete ease.
      She taught me how to wash and iron,

humored all my childish hurts and praised
      my triumphs. I remember once, in tears

over a long-forgotten loss, running to find her
      sheet-whipped between two lines of clothes;

I burrowed my face in her thick skirt. Wet sheets
      buffeting us and a fragrance rose from her body

that comforted me deeply. I had found a font
      of true affection in Mrs. Overhalse, the first

woman I ever heard laugh loudly and vigorously.
      She would throw her head back—her throat,

chin and nose as ruddy as her lips—then, her
      bright eyes, which had all but disappeared

in the flesh of her delight, would return and take me
      into her gaze as if I were her own sweet child:

                     Little Cherub, she'd say.

4

circa 1906–1909

A nurse who attended my children, Blanche
        Spring, for three or so years,
was my only friend. Sympathetic to my clumsy
        attempts at mothering, she
assured me I would grow more confident. I wished,
        later, when the troubles in my children's
lives emerged—their nineteen divorces, nervous
        breakdowns, business failures, and so on—

I had taken her advice and raised them myself,
        but in my family, in that era, such was
unheard of. The children would have led happier
        lives I think, and, as adults,
we would feel closer to one another. Then, too,
        I might not have done some
of the things I was advised by others to do,
        such as encasing James' thumbs

in wire mesh to stop him from sucking on them
        or when Anna was still a small child,
to have her hands tied to the bedposts at night.
        I am certain my mother had the same done
to me. There were special cotton bands for this—
        long enough so the child could turn
safely in her sleep, but not so long that she
        could touch below her navel.

When Franklin first succumbed to his illness,
        there were many days before
a trained nurse could make it north to Campo.
        For three weeks, day and night,

I nursed Franklin competently, although no one
         could have halted the abhorrent
progress of infantile paralysis. When Doctor
         Lovett told me I had kept Franklin alive,
I knew I owed my skill, and his life, to the skills
         Blanche Spring had taught me.

5

To his lasting humiliation, my Grandfather Roosevelt,
  an Abolitionist, paid a substitute
to fight in his place in the Union Army, as did my
  Grandfather Valentine Hall:
two Famine Irish, most likely, more in need
  of the $300 than of their lives,
or so my grandfathers believed. I wonder if either
  substitute made it back to the Port
of New York, or if one or both are buried in ditches
  at Chickamauga or Chancellorsville.
When my brother Hall and my cousin Quentin
  enlisted as aviators during
World War I, having memorized the eye chart
  since neither could see very well,
my grandmother asked why Hall had not hired
  a substitute. To that, I expressed
my first-ever opinion contrary to hers: *Grandmama,*
  I said, with as much indignation
in my voice as I could marshal, *a gentleman is*
  no different from any other kind
of citizen in the United States. It would be a disgrace
  to pay a man to risk his life for you!
Although, when Quentin was killed in aerial
  combat on Bastille Day over France,
I did wish, for a moment, another man had died
  in Quentin's place. Uncle Teddy,
that brusque, brash, bear of a man, my father's
  beloved brother, my once-guardian,
withered from the blow and was gone in a half-year.

6

I was married before I was told that a maid,
Katy Mann, who had attended us in France

the last time my parents and my brothers
and I were ever together, bore a son in 1891

she named Elliott. The son sent congratulations
when Franklin won the presidency. I let him

know I hoped someday we'd meet—then
reconsidered and dropped the connection.

To prevent scandal, Miss Mann had demanded
a large sum, arranged by my Uncle Teddy

three decades earlier, so the son had no right
to expect recognition. Still, I longed to meet

this Elliott, not much older than my father
when he died. Sometimes, abroad, I'd imagine

stumbling upon my lost half-brother, who was,
perhaps, like my father in nature or appearance.

But I never acted. However great the disparity
between the man my father was and the father

who lives on in me, for comfort's sake, I let
truth drift in slow eddies of declining thought.

7

I cannot now remember the name
of the wet nurse we hired,
an immigrant from Central Europe
who spoke a language I had never
heard. I felt a terrible responsibility
toward her baby, although, in faltering
English she assured me she had plenty
for two: she then reached into her blouse
and held out her engorged breast
in a gesture that caused this Puritan
great distress. I visited her tenement
once on the Lower East Side. She
and her husband and four children
shared a single small room. The smell
of lye and cooking fat and the shabbiness
overcame me, and, in the end,
I could not separate her from her
baby, although she pleaded with me
to take her with us to Albany.
I used some private funds to open
a bank account for the baby fed on
the same milk as my Elliott. I stayed
in touch with this mother for several
years, then she disappeared—died
most likely in one of those waves of
infection—cholera, influenza—that,
throughout those years, grazed through
those neighborhoods of squalor and filth.

8

1913 and 1919

When Franklin was appointed
assistant secretary of the Navy,

his boss, Josephus Daniels,
shocked me one day by

practically ordering me to fire
the four white servants, nurse

and governess we brought
to Washington with us. Only

Negroes, he felt, were suited
for servile work. I found his

views quite brutal, although
years later, during the race

riots of 1919, I dismissed
several servants and hired a Negro

cook, butler, kitchenmaid, and
housemaid. Our white servants

were in the house when Franklin
was entertaining Miss Mercer,

and I could not bear to see eyes
that had watched him betray me,

but moreover, I wanted, at last,
to impress my design, not my mother-

in-law's, on the management
of my home, and she had hired,

years before, each of these I let go.

9

When one has servants, you never forget
      that much of your power
           to get things done,

to enjoy your life,
      comes from their labor,
           labor most would not

choose for themselves. You see the human
      cost in the eyes and demeanor
           of the men and women who

are often near-to-hand, or within
      a bell's sounding, a cord's pull.
           That cost puts you at odds

with what enables you. Conflict gnaws
      and grinds at you, although
           you've been trained to brush

it off like a leaf that glides to a patio table.
      Servants' emotions may be masked
           but cannot be entirely hidden;

even if details are unknown, one senses
      complaint, aggravation, the
           preoccupations of personal lives.

They are sick or in love or frightened,
      worried about a child or a parent,
           scheming to obtain some material thing

or an experience they crave. You can feel
        their judgment of you, know they
                gossip and may start harmful rumors.

Such are the aspects, beyond salary
        and board, that make it a demeaning
                business. Since the day's work

is done when the day's work is done—
        and not a moment sooner—
                I am as hidebound as many,

but I choose the work I do. Devotion and
        passionate conviction call my actions forth,
                not another's—or money's—hold on me.

10

Sometimes, from a train or car window
I'll catch a glimpse of someone who looks
dejected and lost, and I'll remember

the emaciated, rag-clad men, women,
and children I saw in the coal mining
counties of West Virginia and Western

Pennsylvania, some so poor they sheltered
in abandoned coke furnaces. Once I watched
a father and mother and their eight children

stumble out of that cold dark oven into
morning light. And I remember the putrid,
crowded, disease-riddled slums of the Lower

East Side my young charges returned home
to, when, not yet twenty, I joined the Junior
League and taught in a settlement house.

I long to sleep when these memories
come to me, or if I imagine I hear again
the manipulative voices of political glad-

handers and fixers, men in backrooms
thick with cigar smoke setting up tit-for-tat
arrangements, the powerless always cut out,

the largest spoils to the most hypocritical.
I know goodwill and compassionate regard
for others ought to prevail; that many work

tirelessly for the greater good, although I am
no longer a naïve idealist: There is no end
to the suffering some will inflict upon

the bodies, minds, and spirits of others.
More than one form of ultimate reality?
Perhaps isolated individual realities

are all we know and true common ground
is an absurdity. Yet, I work everyday
to bring forth an inkling of it. I am only

one person, inadequate, insufficiently educated,
prone to error, with an unforgiving and
impractical heart. October. Through the sheer

window curtains, the glow of late afternoon
sunlight suffuses the room. Yellow roses in
a vase bring the Earth and human love back

to me. Earth and love will endure for some decades,
perhaps even a century beyond my death.
Of this, I am confident, though of nothing else.

Allenswood

11

1899

The education I received
at my English boarding school,
Allenswood, under headmistress

Mademoiselle Souvestre,
was not typical of the education
given girls during that strange

fin de siècle when many
still believed—quite fervently—
that education in the female

caused madness and sterility.
If a woman became rational
and took herself seriously,

the moral instruction
of children would soon fall
to inferiors, and in a single

generation, the social
order would devolve into chaos,
our civilization in ruins.

12

Here was Mademoiselle Souvestre: her brilliant talk
    darting like sunfish through a dappled
summer pond; no subject dull or irrelevant once her
    magnificent intensity bore down upon it.
The daughter of an esteemed French philosopher
    and novelist, her mind and creativity
encouraged since infancy; a radical thinker; a central
    figure among intellectuals; the epitome
of a sophisticated European; an independent, liberal-
    minded woman—now the center
of my youthful worship. I was fifteen when I first
    came to her, she, sixty-eight.

———

Of course it helped, when I arrived, that I was fluent
    in French. All our classes, except
Shakespeare, were conducted in French, and if
    any girl spoke even a single English
word during the day, she must confess the crime
    that evening when we filed into
Mademoiselle's library for our goodnight kiss.

———

She was rather short and stout. Her snow-white
    hair formed a widow's peak above
a broad forehead then moved back in waves
    to a low, full twist. She held each girl

in her gaze for a moment before she offered her kiss,
    her clear blue eyes seeming to

see into your Soul. Fortunately, she pronounced me
     pur d'espirit et pur le coeur.

————————

I stopped being the silly, frightful, rigid young
        thing I was when Aunt Tissy and I
set sail that last September of the nineteenth
        century. Finally I had a healthy
appetite and no headaches. The proudest day
        of my life became the day I made
first team in field hockey. We took dozens of hard
        blows and played all winter on that cold
mist-shrouded field. I became quite confident—
        a confidence I lost much of in the early
years of marriage—but it came back in my late thirties.

————————

We took history classes in Mademoiselle Souvestre's
        library, a charming room lined
with books and filled with flowers and art on
        the walls—including nudes, which
we were afraid to stare at lest another see our
        curiosity. The windows looked out
on a large expanse of lawn and shade trees that
        became perches and crannies for rooks
in winter. Mademoiselle stood before a large map
        and lectured on the wars and
the political alliances that shaped the beginning
        and end of nations, the heroes

and moral issues, the art and literature of each era.
        She spoke of the French Revolution,
the rise and fall of Napoleon, the Franco-Prussian
        War, and the current-day Boer War

the English were fighting. She was opposed to
    colonial domination of smaller countries—
not a safe view to hold in Wimbledon at the time.

———————

I felt let into a cave full of the gold and jewels
    of empires, and given the vision
to see they were worthless unless a nobler, more
    decent future came into existence.
Wonder, fury, and sorrow flooded me. I felt
    the shifting warp and weft of all human
striving and my own small existence weaving itself
    into history's imposing tapestry.

———————

Best were those red-letter days when Mademoiselle
    gathered a few around her
to read to us French stories, plays, and poems.
    Her voice, low and soft, and quite dramatic,
carried us off on dreams of adventure and romance.

Once, as one of six girls on chairs around
the fire, Mademoiselle in the center, the gold haze
    of gaslight and firelight suffusing
the room, I stared at the broad planes of her face,
    her moving lips, the light and shadow
on the silver waves of her hair, the drape of her skirt,
    transfixed by the sound
and power of words, by her desire that each of us
    live a bold and impassioned life.
I thought to reach out and pluck what she strove
    to give. Although at times my will
was completely subverted, I took that fruit she
    proffered so lovingly. She, and she alone,

is the source of any good I have ever done anyone,
	or my country, or the larger world.

————————

During holidays, at only seventeen, I became
	Mademoiselle Souvestre's traveling
companion. We grew quite close journeying to Paris,
	then Marseilles, down the Mediterranean
coast to Pisa, Florence, Rome. In Florence, she came
	upon me once, my Baedeker open
at a description of the Campanile. *My dear,* she said,
	*the only way to know a city is to walk
its streets.* Alone I wandered that city with its rich
	flavor of antiquity. Reading Dante,
laboriously, I had plenty of imagination to draw upon.
	Every scene, every face became
a part of the Eternal pageant. Even though I became
	quite lost in the narrow streets,
those hours were glorious. I wandered toward whatever
	called to me from curiosity or beauty,
and I came to love the world and feeling alive and free.

————————

Many of Mademoiselle's fascinating and impressive
	friends, both men and women,
appeared at dinner, which, at Allenswood, was always
	formal. Since I was a favorite, some said
her favorite of favorites, I often sat at table directly
	across from Mademoiselle, where
I learned a great deal eavesdropping on her exchanges
	with artists, philosophers, political
leaders, novelists, poets. I picked up the habit of asking
	leading questions; then, using a few scraps

of facts and the new words I heard in answer,
    would appear to know more than I knew.
When I was first lady, and later, a delegate to
    the United Nations, then ambassador-
at-large, this habit served me well, although I lived
    in dread of others discovering that,
often, I understood an issue only superficially.
    This is cleverness, and oh yes,
I can, at times, be quite clever. Mademoiselle,
    you see, still admonishes me from Heaven—
Toddy, tu te conduis mesquinement. Ça par exemple!

Marriage
& Family

13

1907

A few years after Franklin and I married,
my mother-in-law hired Charles A. Platt
to design Siamese-twin brownstones

on Sixty-Fifth Street. We had a common
entryway, her door to the left, ours to
the right. Mama insisted on pocket doors;

doors opened onto four of our house's
five floors, thus she would appear,
a white revenant in her sleeping robe

at night, or, any hour of the day,
corseted and brusquely intrusive.
I never felt free. One evening I began

sobbing and could not stop. *You've gone
quite mad, Eleanor!* Franklin fumed.
I simply couldn't abide living one more

instant in a home I had not chosen.
Why hadn't you raised the matter sooner?
For God's sake! For Pity's sake!

But I was dutiful—duty was all I knew.
I complied. I acquiesced. I adjusted.
I seldom raised objections. But then

I brooded, schemed, undertook
subterfuge, worked behind the scenes,
became a covert manipulator of emotions,

qualities in me that, over the years,
served Franklin, the politician,
even as they infuriated the man.

14

1909

Our third child was born in my fourth
year of marriage, born in three hours,
but with no less pain than Anna or James—
a perfect flower of a child—eleven pounds.
He would bear his father's name.

Six months later we christened him
in Saint James' Episcopal Church
where Franklin and Franklin's father
were christened, where, on Franklin's side,
all Roosevelts dedicated their own to Christ.

Weeks later, at seven months and fourteen
days, we buried Baby Franklin in the graveyard
at Saint James'. Rosy and Sean McGuire
slowly lowered that tiny brass coffin.
Scrape-scratch, shovel to gravelly earth.

Thud-thunk as earth hit brass. Surely,
I thought, I would fade away.
Scrape-scratch. Thud-thunk.
I stopped eating as baby had.
The rack of guilt. The rack of grief.

My baby had cried and gasped
and coughed faint broken coughs
through those last dreadful nights
and days: his pulse raced, slowed,
raced, slowed, stopped—an infection

of the heart. A Soul had passed
through me I never knew, for I'd handed
him off, as I so often had, to a servant
or his nurse. From November to spring,
I woke up wailing to whoever attended me—

We must get baby out of the ground.
He's alive; I know he is. He'll freeze
if we don't get him out. Help me.
Help me. Please, please, help me.

All my life I came back to Saint
James' and stood before my baby's
small marker near a stone wall
and a cypress tree. Mornings
an orange light would glow reflected

off the back of the church, then beyond,
the dark Hudson and the first
bluish-purple ridges of the Catskills.
The terror of being buried alive never
left me. Fifty years later, so I wouldn't

wake in the cold bitter dark, as I was
sure Baby had, I begged my doctor,
David Gurewitsch, to have my carotid
artery severed after the coroner certified
death, and David promised he would.

15

My mother-in-law furnished our house,
hired and dismissed our servants,
assumed care and authority for the children,
which I, in my naïveté and insecurity,
surrendered to her. She told them
I am your real mother—Eleanor
merely bore you. When I did dare
a decision, she found fault every time.
Soon I stopped speaking, stopped thinking...

In the snarls and knots of my hours,
I crawled, lost in a stranger's nightmare.
Six times in ten years I carried a child
and gave birth—my social function.
I never questioned the given order,
what was and what was not done
by a woman in my position. You see,
through the early years of my marriage,
I was not yet a person, not a true person.

Betrayal

16

1918

Shipboard from Great Britain to New York,
    Franklin stood on the icy deck

for each ceremony, caught pneumonia
    and that ravaging influenza near

the end of the War. The remains of forty-three
    sailors and officers were each sheet-

wrapped, bound, commended to the depths
    and to God, then slid into the cold

dark Atlantic. Once he was ours again,
    to spare others infection, I unpacked

his valise, how I came to find a packet
    of letters, each in a threaded, ivory

envelope inscribed in a delicate hand I knew—
    a family friend's, my social secretary's—

Lucy Mercer's. I had harbored suspicions.
    Now the iron brace of dread that had

pressed ever tighter against my body,
    fell away, and with it, came a momentary

queasy elation. Like a panther that creeps on its
    haunches then sits before it strikes,

I paused, then slid each from its envelope, spread
    it open. Facts have about them a devil-

may-care indifference—and I would have the facts.

———

We were in the Sixty-Fifth Street house, so I walked
    to the small paneled study off
the first-floor west wing, locked the door. Trying
    to untie the string wound round the packet
of letters, my hands shook like cold chicks shake.
    Franklin and Lucy's passion raveled
the cursive line, and I took their unholy love
    into my body like a communion wafer
dipped in arsenic, then sat there unmoving.
    The opened letters on the desktop, caught
in the lamp's amber light, shone like the tips
    of bright sails. Finally, I struggled upstairs,
my knees folding under me twice, then,
    so no one would hear me, I wept into
my pillow, a long weeping that wracked me
    so hard, my back burned for days,
my breastbone a dividing wedge that spiked
    with pain each time a single phrase
came back to me of what Lucy had written.

———

He had taken her out driving
                through long afternoons
        in the Virginia countryside—
forays that ended in teasing seductions.

                Lucy unwound
        the details playfully:
Franklin's praising her face, her thighs,
                back, and breasts,

her graceful motions, his awe
                        at how sweetly
she welcomed his advances.

            Again and again, Lucy
        said what had been   mine alone to say—
            my darling, my truest heart.
I could see him
                    in that straw hat
            he wears cocked to the side,
        his radiant smile,
                        hear his hearty laughter
and that murmur
        he makes when he's kissed.

            And she?
        She's in navy polka dots on white chenille,
            a large lace collar,
                    her black curls tied back
                        in a red ribbon.

                ———

I offered Franklin his freedom of course.
        Mama and I, and Franklin, sick
as he was, spoke in the parlor that next afternoon.
        A solemn conference. She said
she would cut him off without a cent. He would not
        inherit Springwood, and she reminded
him Miss Mercer was a Catholic and could never
        marry a divorced man.
Later, Louie Howe confirmed for him the certain
        demise of a political future . . .
I held all the cards, the cards for a world demolished.
        What I required was his

pledge he would never again see her. He agreed,
        our gaze locking for an instant.
Did I ever again look so deeply into him, or see
        his eyes? I think not. I could not
have borne the connivance I would have found there.

———————

He had a mistress. I was betrayed as Father
        had betrayed Mother. I who had borne
six of his children, one of them dead. Motherhood
        and social obligations had confounded me,
stripped me of any sense of the self-possession
        I had so tenuously acquired at Allenswood.
Now this—for which no mannered grace or lessons
        in protocol had prepared me. A quick,
deep rending, a buckshot shattering of all the birds
        that bound the sky of my dreams.
That night, in the dark, after declining a call
        to dinner and another to kiss
the kiddles goodnight, I felt a dark sorrow rise
        above me like a shadow, then watched
as that sorrow settled down on my bones,
        an icy lover who never rose.

———————

We returned to the house on N Street, five children
        and four servants in tow.
Appearances returned to normal, although I could
        neither command my body
to enter the room he slept in, nor permit him to enter
        mine. Both of us disconsolate . . .

———

I lived in a world where infidelity was committed
    by inferior human beings
only, not by a person living as Franklin had lived,
    in a sanctified state. So who was
he now? This was a tangle of irreconcilable truths.
    One lives with them because
one lives, because God tries us and finds us wanting.

———

Revulsion and rage drained me, but what sickened
    me most was that I had yearned
desperately for such an easy intimacy as was theirs,
    only I believed Franklin was
incapable of giving what he so joyfully gave Lucy.
    Why had he never given me
as much? Something tainted and shrunken in me
    failed to call forth such
a response in him. I cursed myself and believed
    my flaws made me utterly unlovable.

Aftermath

17

1919

I was alone on my thirty-fifth birthday,
if any woman with five children is ever alone.

A topaz dawn dissolved to a scintillant
blue sky, a clear October day.

The two youngest were in the nursery
with Blanche. The door to the summer kitchen
    slammed, then slammed again.

      Servants about their business.

Otis was cranking the car.
It sputtered and backfired three times.

I was a familiar drudge, plodding through duties,
bound by purposes defined by others.

I looked up from my writing desk
to the walled back courtyards of R Street,
and thought of Saint-Gaudens' statue, *Grief,*
as she sits in Rock Creek Cemetery,
hidden in a grove of holly and laurel,
the dark green leaves leathery and tatty.

Franklin was off to hunt in New Brunswick,
the Campo house opened to accommodate
him and six companions. I imagined the men
sitting before the fieldstone chimney after dinner,

enveloped in cigar smoke, amber whiskey
glinting in firelight, Franklin's voice loudest

among a raucous trumping of speculations
and gossip, the certain recounting of the week's
proud kills—moose, elk, deer, fox, quail.

Then I heard myself sighing, heard sorrow
and a long and tiresome loneliness rise up
from my diaphragm and release through
my mouth. This is what I do. I sigh.

Buck up, I heard Uncle Teddy intone brusquely.
Buck up, you silly goose.

O yes, I thought, I am a goose of a woman—
my long neck, my steep-sloping shoulders,
six feet of lofty, homely awkwardness.

I have been a shy goose among more practical fowl.

But I began that instant—although every moment
of my upbringing was against it—to care less
for the success of my husband's projects,
                    and more for the success of my own.

18

1921

There was that messy business
Franklin got himself into
the last year he was assistant
secretary of the Navy—

the Newport Sex Scandal.
How naïve we were before
the Roaring Twenties!
Franklin was determined

to clean up vice in a town
where thousands of sailors
were in port—some visiting
houses of ill-repute, trafficking

in cocaine, gambling, and
engaging in what the papers
called *a nameless perversion*.
He issued an order permitting

undercover agents to go
to the limit to obtain evidence.
When a highly esteemed
local chaplain was entrapped,

it all came crashing down
on poor Franklin's head.
All reports had come to him,
you see; all funds from his office.

When called before the Naval
Board of Inquiry, Franklin
said he'd never given a thought
as to how his order would be

carried out. A physician
and a detective trained a dozen
volunteer sailors how to spot
likely perverts and how they

should act to lure them. Young
men dated, seduced, and were
sodomized in the name of duty,
thereby, the Board claimed,

the Navy had corrupted its
own men. Franklin assumed,
as I would have, that the men
might hide under a bed

or look over a transom, not
that they would become
participants in the act itself.
Seventeen entrapped sailors

were court-martialed—most were
imprisoned. Thus Franklin's
political career may have ended
before it truly began. He was

outraged and anxious of course,
and denounced the report in
strenuous terms . . . And he may
have used his political leverage

and private funds to tamp down
coverage in the national press.
Whether Washington officials knew
or not, immoral acts were committed

on immoral orders, and for years
after that, whenever I'd catch myself
watching one of my own four boys
growing into a man before my eyes,

a man who might enlist one day,
I'd remember those young men
who surrendered peace of mind
and the sanctity of their bodies

on the order of a commanding officer.

19

1921

When Franklin became ill, he was struck first
    with chills, weakness, exhaustion,
then paralysis moved up from his feet to his knees,

then his thighs, back, across his abdomen, and even,
    at one point, to his arms and hands.
I dared not show him my terror or warm to the dread

that held a wall of ice against me. My lungs seemed
    to shred themselves against my ribcage;
at times, I could barely breathe. He could neither

urinate nor move his bowels. I knew he would feel
    humiliated if anyone else
catheterized him, or gave him an enema, and that

he would die if I did not do these things. And so,
    remembering everything the children's
nurse, Blanche Spring, taught me, I did. I bathed

and shaved him, brushed his teeth, emptied his bedpan,
    removed his soiled sheets, wiped his legs
and buttocks, turned him again and again to prevent

infection. I was most intimate with him in these ways,
    the first time I had touched him
since he had betrayed me. This man I had not yet

let back into my heart, was now, again, my heart's
    sole object, the focus of all my thought.
Franklin, then thirty-nine, had always thrown his body

into every act, an athletic man who, just a few
        days before, had swum and sailed,
and, with the children, torn down pine boughs

and beaten back a brush fire. The year before,
        at the Democratic Convention in San
Francisco, he'd leaped from a stage and wrenched

the New York State banner from Tammany boss
        Murphy then led the delegates in a rousing
parade through the hall. He'd been rewarded with

his party's nomination for vice president and run
        an extremely arduous campaign on behalf
of James Cox, traveling through much of our country,

more the happier warrior than Al Smith had ever been.
        Now here he lay unable to roll his body over,
to bend his knees, or control his most basic functions,

and while Franklin must have felt terrified, he never
        once expressed fear or self-pity.
If he felt betrayed by his body, or Fate, or God,

he never said so. He was kindness and gratitude
        itself . . . *Thank you, dear Babs*, he'd say,
and in the sweetest of voices, *That's so good of you dear*

when I'd done any of the dozens of tasks that filled
        my days and nights. I slept on the couch
a few feet away in that small upstairs bedroom where

this horrendous drama, our great crisis unfolded.
        I sat hour after hour in a window seat—
only the view of a low hill, pines, and sky brought

me solace. The incongruity between these private,
       and for me, severely trying moments
and my knowledge of Franklin's flamboyant personality,

a man regarded as a *bon vivant*, astounded me.
       I bore witness to the spirit and the flesh,
appearance and reality, all one must weigh and measure.

Was he a prince lifted up high and brought down low, I'd think,
       then correct myself, or a tenderhearted
and vulnerable man ennobled because he embraces

ill-fortune with a generous spirit? I saw how love
       would have its way; not one's favored
or wished-for way, but its singular and mysterious way.

20

I do not advocate the way Franklin handles
        personal feelings he would
rather not deal with. Convinced that anything
        ignored for a sufficient time
resolves itself, when emotions threaten to
        turn disagreeable, he leaves
the room turning to say, *you will feel*
        differently when you calm down,
or *you are looking at this in the wrong light.*
        Although it is horrid to feel
all bottled up, I do think it essential,
        at times, to force one's self to not
think of certain things. We both inherited
        the legacy of self-containment
our daughter, Anna, railed against. It makes
        true intimacy impossible
for one must never admit to feeling helpless
        or weak. I could be every bit
as controlled, when need be, as Franklin was.
        This was the Roosevelt way:
individuals of superior breeding must never
        in public, and rarely in private,
let bubbling vats of maggoty rage, or sorrow,
        or dread or frustration, come
to the surface. Fearless, confident, and cheerful:
        always the order of the day.

21

The day I drove her from Hyde Park
to Cornell, my sullen, sulking,
silent daughter pressed her body

against the car door as if to say
I was anathema. I counted
my motherly sins of commission,

my motherly sins of omission:
a considerable count, doubtless
thousands forgotten. I pleaded

with God for forgiveness, for guidance,
although I could not then forgive
my mother-in-law for her unrelenting

interference in my children's lives.
She bribed them with money and gifts
freely, and, at times, strenuously

opposed Franklin's and my wishes.
The day before, Mama told Anna
she'd become a spinster if she went

to college, that *a bookish girl is
terribly unattractive.* My grandmother
and godmothers believed this as well;

thus my own formal education ended
at seventeen. That I hadn't attended
Vassar or Barnard, as many New York

women of my generation and class
had, was a great loss to me. Raising
children is perhaps an impossible

task, yet so often, walking down a street
or before falling asleep, I'd imagine
reliving that day, seeing that golden

September landscape flowing round us
and still miles from Cornell, Anna as far
from me as her lanky frame permitted,

her eyes hidden behind a swag of blond
hair, and, somehow, I'd smash
my righteousness, my stubborn will,

until my stoical heart broke open:
*My dear darling, my magnificent girl,
my precious Anna, I love you beyond*

all measure. This I'd say over and again,
tears stinging me blind until I'd stop,
turn the roadster around, and bring her home.

Friends
& Lovers

22

Brilliant blue-sky days and deep green pines—
and the sea!—glorious to behold on Campo,

yet I loved fogbound days as well when
a delicate beauty felt as near as a goddess

to the Greeks. I liked to hear the wind whistle
and howl in the eaves, a comforting sound

to me, as if I were held dear by a tremendous
soothing force. There might be children

running in and out, crying fiercely a minute
or two over a scraped knee or toy or trinket

claimed by another, but these were momentary
disruptions. Oh but I was happy on Campo!—

Mama in her own cottage down the road
or off to Europe for the summer, Franklin

rarely returning since the summer of his
paralysis. Esther, Marion, Nancy, and Caroline

visiting—or any mix of a dozen women friends
over the years. We would breakfast on the patio

immersed in the atmosphere of island, garden,
sea, and sunshine, linger in conversation

for two or three hours, nothing more planned
than a trip to the grocer or a walk around

the pond. Sometimes we gathered mussels
with the children and their friends after we

swam and had taken a few hours to write and
read or sleep. Inevitably Nan would start

the giggles going round, and then laughter
was irrepressible. We were keen in our views

on this cause or that, or for a novel or play,
and we loved to gossip and reminisce.

We would tease whoever was gloomiest
until she broke and put irritation aside.

Women in our late thirties, our forties,
and then our fifties—woman conspiring

under conditions of privilege and isolation,
of great natural beauty and abundance,

and usually, in glorious weather—
women at our peak, at the full of life,

women who knew too well that *in back
of tranquility lies always conquered unhappiness.*

23

1929

If I was going to inspect institutions
and public works, I wanted to drive
my own car. I refused to be chauffeured
about in a limousine, so Franklin
assigned Corporal Miller, a state
trooper, to guard and escort me.

Hour after hour, a day or two a week,
as we drove around a lake or through
a valley, quite naturally, we drew
into conversation. I sensed, as perhaps
only another orphan would, the depths
and hollows of Earl's shielded loneliness.

Kin of the same heart,
although not of the same social class,
I offered him the solace of my friendship.
He offered me the solace of his.

We covered quite a bit of territory,

and after I told him of Franklin
and Lucy Mercer, we grew closer.

We spoke until we emptied ourselves
of our histories and then we simply looked—
at eyes, lips, hands, the way a body
carries itself as it moves across a room.

24

1929

I was at war with myself   for the visions of Earl's
body that would leave me
        awash at a window   or frozen
   at the threshold of a door   I was unable

to sit still in my bath   or to lie still in my bed
or be in any one place for more than a minute or two
       without feeling my legs about to carry me off
  fire burning slowly across the plains and hills of my skin

      not only had I absorbed every scintilla
of Grandmother Hall's prudery
      but for eleven years I clung to my
indignation   my self-righteousness over Franklin's infidelity
and now I was

        about to commit adultery—
with a man a dozen years   younger than I was
  a man not of my class   nor of my station
    my children's mother

    Sara Roosevelt's daughter-in-law
a Ludlow-Livingston-Hall Roosevelt
    the first lady of the Empire State
        a Roosevelt twice over . . .

25

Earl touched my body
with such reverence,
oh my lady, he said,
my dear, dear lady

and my pulse raced
with the joy of it. I think,
too, driving on those rough
roads stimulated my body

so as to render me
especially sensitive to
touch. When I did succumb—
after having passed through

the lobby of an out-of-the-way
hotel, my face hidden beneath
a broad-brimmed hat—
all the repression and wariness,

the long stuffed down and sat
upon, welled up and burst.
I gave Earl the charge blaster—
but I let myself explode.

26

Franklin would succeed in the election,
almost anyone would have opposing
Hoover—and divorce, occurring after
he assumed office—well the disgrace
would blow over, certainly, before
he stood for re-election. Since I'd marry
Earl as soon as possible, the president
would be seen as the injured party.
I wouldn't have minded the infamy
on my head alone, but then, what kind
of citizen surrenders the opportunity,
through her proximity to a president,
of doing some real good? I was frozen:
a rabbit in a rifle's sight. And Earl,
ever protective, and in these matters,
cunning—my Knight Errant, my *chevalier*—
to quell rumors running through
the barrooms and bedrooms of Albany,
had proposed to Ruth Bellinger.
Against Mama's objections, I was
arranging his wedding at Hyde Park.

Over the years, after Ruth, Earl divorced
and married two more times, and most
regrettably, after Franklin's death,
when I was, in a sense, the nation's widow,
his third wife, seeking her divorce, named
me a co-conspirator to Earl's infidelity—
one occasion I was grateful I carried
the Roosevelt name—and that, by then,

I could direct my income through
discreet channels. His wife was given
custody of their two children, a girl
named Eleanor and a boy named Earl,
and I've always hoped she set aside
that settlement for their education.

27

Earl's love forced me to overcome the barrier
of age, and the barrier of class, and then,
reflected in his brown eyes, I felt, at last,
I was something of a beauty. When he touched
me or gently urged my body in this direction
or that, I felt strong and sleek as an otter.
He drew the compass of my senses. Once,
in one of the dozens of seaside villages
we escaped to for a weekend—two late
diners on an outdoor patio, two anonymous,
everyday lovers—with tears in his eyes,
whispering in his deep voice, the words
coming slowly—he said, *You are a great
woman, dear lady, whose destiny I was
born to serve with every ounce of my strength.*
I let his words show me who he saw me to be,
and I thought of Mademoiselle Souvestre
all those evenings long ago in England
when we schoolgirls sat about her in her parlor
and she read to us: how radiant she was
and how I longed for her to look up
and smile at me. The deep confidence
she bred in me returned through
the extraordinary men and women I came
to know and admire. My closest women
friends, and Earl, Louie Howe, and Lorena
of course, for I could not admire myself,
and perhaps, truly love myself, until I saw
how they saw me, and felt how they loved me.

28

Earl and I were Lady and Knight Errant,
    a reality that transcended time and form.
We had simply to accede to this truth
    as evidenced in our hearts. I know
there is an element of the romantic and even
    the fantastical in this view, but nothing
has ever enabled me as knowing this has.
    The world of appearances is handled easily
when the world of substance, the Soul's
    realm, is before you. I discovered this
as a lonely child when I would climb a tree
    at Tivoli to read the stories of Walter Scott,
and I agree, in the way of literature, Scott's stories
    shaped me, and they shaped Earl. The outward
scene became chaotic over time. I cannot count
    the women, often dancers or actresses, and heavy
drinkers, a few rather uncouth, Earl brought
    to Val-Kill, not to mention his three wives.
He accepted my peculiarities and the demands
    of my position, and we never stopped enjoying
one another's company. What mattered most
    was he needed me, and I needed his loyalty.

29

1932

She's all yours, Hickok. Have fun!
the city editor called out to Lorena

when he assigned her to cover me—
the nominee's wife—that autumn

of the first presidential campaign.
An AP reporter, one of only a few

women journalists, perhaps the only
one who held her own among those

poker-playing, hard-drinking, rough-
mannered men of the National Press Corp—

one of the guys—but a woman to me.
The harrowing, grueling months

of campaigning, the unending waves
of dread and despair that arose in me,

through it all, there was Hick,
Hicky-Doddles, Lorena Hickok,

the rumored illegitimate granddaughter
of Wild Bill. I pursued her, I do admit—

and she—well, she rescued me. Without
Hick, I would not have dared one tenth

of what I dared accomplish as first lady.
She was my spark, my cache of gunpowder.

Bosom buddies—bosom, belly, thighbone
buddies—buddies from head to toe.

30

1932 and onward

Hick was glorious company and now
that Earl was married, I was lonely.
We traveled to Arizona and through
the Midwest, thousands of miles

on board that train in the weeks
leading up to the November election.
I liked to challenge her to keep up with
me. Once we ran through a cornfield

in Iowa together, and I had to rescue
her from the barbed wire fence that
snagged her. I snagged her. From
across my stateroom car, she'd smile

so sweetly at me, immense tenderness
in her eyes. In those moments our eyes
caught, I felt we shared a common heart.
Both of us lost our mothers as children,

and while I'd lost my adoring father,
her crude father had tormented and
overworked her, and once, in a rage, smashed
her only comfort, a kitten, against a wall.

Hick fled from him at fourteen after
he raped and beat her. I wanted to
comfort her and comfort myself in her.
I admired her compassion for the world's

downtrodden, her righteous rage
against injustice. She enlarged
and bolstered me, although I see
we were two motherless women

in love, each caring for, in the other,
her own sweet child, strengthening
one another until we were as brave
as we would ever be, and as happy.

31

Ares sent the Depression then War; Eros, Passion;
and since no form of love should be despised,
I did not turn but returned love in my fashion.

Although Hick had my deepest heart, her ration
of my time was cut and cut again, compromised
when Ares sent the Depression and War, Eros Passion.

One plays a role in public when one has to win
backing for this or that issue—I could strategize—
and did!—not turning, but loving in my fashion.

It was service to others, to causes, turned love ashen
after bright first blazings died—or were excised.
Ares sent the Depression then War; Eros, Passion.

My hard-driving reporter with skywide compassion
for the downtrodden, my advisor (wise or unwise)—
I did not turn but loved you in my fashion.

And while whirligig time is never de-rationed,
I haven't a thought of you, a kiss, a touch, I'd revise;
although Ares sent Depression then War; Eros, Passion,
I did not turn but loved you in my fashion.

32

Years later, when Lorena and I would take
off incognito to drive through the Canadian
Rockies or across the country to camp out
at Lake Roosevelt, I'd feel again how grateful
I was to Earl. He taught me to drive fearlessly,
and with speed, to shoot a pistol, dive,
sing with a light heart, to laugh and eat
with gusto. A little of his pleasure in living
rubbed off on me: before Earl, I had never
known a single person who seemed to genuinely
delight in being alive. With Lorena, I treasured
her brilliant mind and the way my intellect shone
in the light of hers. Lorena's belief in my capacity
to carry off, and with aplomb, the role of first lady,
enabled me to do some actual good, I think.
She persuaded me to hold press conferences
in the White House for the women of the press corps,
and my late-at-night letters to Hick and hers to me,
at least the portions of them suitable for the public,
evolved into my daily syndicated column,
My Day, and into my books, such as *It's Up
to the Women*. The column, books, and articles,
and my speeches, allowed me to reach, and teach,
and at times persuade, hundreds of thousands,
if not millions. I never lost a feeling of kinship
for anyone who is suffering, but translating feelings
into action, and then into policy, into laws that
guaranteed economic security, housing, health,
freedom, and so much more . . . Well, I wasn't
the president, I merely had privileged access
to a president. I did what I could continuously
and persistently, but it was Lorena's ideas,

and mine that emerged with her—these, and her
sweet smile, tender heart, her faith in me, her love,
in those early White House years, that saved my life.

33

During the 1932 campaign, the public
formed an impression of me as viewed through
Hick's adoring eyes—and I adored her pale green
eyes, her soft lips, the comfort and pleasure
that bound us more deeply every time we shared
a bed. While we knew Franklin ridiculed us—
referring to Hick as *my missus' she-man*—
we cared less, humming together in our brilliant
affinities. Her wry, and even at times, ribald humor,
when I could ease up a little, made her fabulous
company. And her grumpy manner, her great need
for affection, called to the mother in me. To treasure
her fully was the one thing I could do. Of course,
Lorena wanted more of me, and in that regard,
I was hindered by my public role and my family's
needs. I gave what I could, but she gave me more.

34

Sometimes, beside David on a plane or in a car,
     the yearning to be younger
than I am would overtake me: a burning first
     at the base of my throat
that spread quickly, then a penetrating chill.
     Yes, I have wished we were
more than we are—stouthearted traveling
     companions, dearest friends,
true confidants—but the physical satisfactions
     of youth or even hearty middle age,
had passed. Simply being a younger Eleanor,
     would not, in itself, be enticement
enough for a true lady's man, and David was that.
     This seriously weak chin,
the most obvious of my physical disappointments;
     my protruding teeth;
this voice that runs to the most irritating registers
     of sound; no, none of that
would have appealed to him. Yet, should she wish,
     and oh I did!—a slope-bellied
old mule of a woman can dream, quite vibrantly,
     for she's known truly
the heft and drive of a young man's body moving
     over and through her.

35

Once, in 1948, David and I had two days in Zurich.
Romantic illusions whirled through my mind
like dozens of spinning tops: I thought he'd say . . .
and want . . . and do . . . I bristled with anticipation.

David had booked rooms for us at the Dolder,
and quite coincidentally, his lover and her husband
were booked there as well, and in a room next
to his; my room on his other side. He never

knew I knew, but I am sensitive to these things,
and occasions brought the four of us into the same
sphere. This sent spinning dreams to a slow
wobbling halt. Where does this capacity of mine

to recalibrate expectations come from? My heart's
ratcheting mechanism—it ratchets up, it ratchets
down—one more gift from my alcoholic father?
One ages into unvarnished facts, ages into a realist.

36

Before I bore six children, I cut quite the figure.
      Long, strong arms and legs—
an athletic form truly—and for most of my life,
      the stamina of an athlete.
When walking alone my quick stride elated me:
      the liquefactions of skirt,
slip, stockings moving over thighs and knees.
      Head up! Shoulders back!
March! I would command myself, and oh did
      I fly down the street.
David always kept apace, although I suppose,
      because he is my junior by
two decades, I should say I kept apace
      of David. It is not
simply his beauty, his form, that catches
      my drowsy breath—
it is his bearing and disposition, the innate
      grace of an intelligent,
worldly man. And David endures my foibles,
      my sulks and temper,
my envy—first of his intimate relations
      and later of his wife, Edna.
Long ago I realized the prudent thing was
      to always love the ones
my lovers loved, and, for the most part, I have.

37

The truth is never wholly palatable: David is
     more my son than any of my four,
and he regards me in a motherly frame. That is
     not as I wish, but age does extract
its requirements, and the flesh, oh the flesh,
     given the gravitas of time,
given the gravity of space . . . and then
     I know where my grave will be,
I see it and see what there is to see in the grave.
     Like a creature burrowing—
a constant mole—Eternity scratching near.

38

Should Fate ever permit me to choose just one,
to be again as young as I was when I chose
Franklin, I would choose David instead.
I love him as I have never loved anyone.
Ironical that he should come to me after
Franklin, Earl, and Lorena, after the children
have disappeared into their lives, and into
their children's lives. Yes, I am a grandmother
many times over, a widow, Ambassador
Extraordinaire, *First Lady of the World*
Truman called me—can you imagine?
Yet, I would forego all accolades, all
opportunities, to be first in David's life alone.
Foolishness, I know, but my truth, and since
it lives like a hermit crab in me, enshelled,
unshared, almost—not quite—unspoken,
I'll hold onto this instead of holding him.

A Politician's Wife /
First Lady

39

I have known only a few very happy marriages,
and while certainly Franklin's affair began
my disillusionment about my own, I did not
give up hope immediately. By happy marriage

I do not mean two people who get along
together and live contentedly, but those few
who are excitingly happy—who find joy
in one another's company. Some of Franklin's

actions, over the years, led me to surmise
there was something truly implacable in him,
that certain sympathies, important to me,
and important, I would venture, to all men

and women of goodwill, would never arise
in him. This is a harsh indictment, and I say
this despite knowing his struggle with
infantile paralysis did, in some regards,

and at times, act to deepen his compassion.

40

late 1932 / early 1933

When I think of those months
between the nomination and the first
inaugural, I think first of flying
through a day and night in a Ford

Tri-Motor, the propellers' drone,
the vibration, the rumble of wind
over fuselage and wings—every muscle
of my body stiffened against becoming

a prisoner of the White House.
I knew I would stand hour upon hour,
day upon day, grinning an automaton's
grin, mouthing words of welcome,

of flattery, my mind deadened
by small talk, my time and spirit
conceded to others. The solicitous,
bedecked, cheerful Mrs. Roosevelt—

I despised her—she who I would
pretend to be. The feast of my private
life, fought for so fiercely and at great
cost, would, as first lady, shrivel

to less than a biscuit of hardtack.
We flew from Albany to Chicago
the day after the convention's fourth
ballot went to Franklin: He and his

secretary, Missy LeHand,
his bodyguard, Gus Gennerich,
my secretary, Grace Tully,
and Earl and I—civilian air flight

in its infancy, headwinds tremendous.

41

As we were leaving Albany to fly to Chicago
so Franklin might accept his party's nomination
on the convention's floor—an unprecedented

act—he told me he had cut a deal with William
Randolph Hearst, that broker of elections,
agreeing to abandon the World Court

and the League of Nations for his editorial
support. My husband sacrificed his principles
for power, for both of us believed,

and had worked ardently for many years,
on this issue: that the Court and the League
were our best hopes for preventing another

world war. And for several years after that,
when many were crying out for legislation
that would make the barbaric lynching

of our Negro brothers a federal crime,
Franklin refused, repeatedly, his support,
letting one bill after another die an ignominious

death. His refusal on this, and on other worthy
proposals—because he would not stand up
to the Dixiecrats—because he enjoyed calling

himself *a practical politician*—was cowardice.
My heart ached over these actions and non-
actions of his. I'd do what I could to persuade

him otherwise, then I would close my eyes
and pray, and with all my might, will him
to act otherwise. Sometimes, then, I'd feel

gratitude to Miss Mercer, for his affair broke
the spell of my enthrallment to Franklin
sustained in the early years of our marriage.

Without this inadvertent gift of his cupidity,
I could not have endured. I was free: thus
his high-handedness, callousness, ignominy,

when they shone forth, never imperiled my Soul.

42

1932

Visible from the small window of the plane
carrying us to Chicago, the farms and villages
of New York. They appeared as the peaceable
kingdom, an Eden flowing below me. Then,

with nightfall, sparks or bracelets of light
around a lake or along the course of a river,
before the long dark of the Alleghenies.
When Franklin first sought the nomination,

I was unhappy, although it was for him
a tremendous triumph over adversity;
but Earl and I had been lovers for three years—
I could not endure the public pretense

a moment longer. The children were grown.
I was forty-seven, weary of being dutiful,
weary of caring, weary of my sons' ill-regard.
Crossing the enormous dark of Lakes Erie

and Michigan, Earl and I together near the back,
Franklin and the others before us in the trembling,
rumbling plane, to comfort myself, I repeated
the words Christ spoke at Gethsemane:

My soul is exceeding sorrowful, even unto
death. Then I leaned into Earl and whispered,
Tarry ye here, and watch with me. He squeezed
my hand and raised it to his lips and kissed it.

I drew back and took up my dread and held
it close, and into the dark of that unbearable
night quietly said, *O my Father, if it be
possible, let this cup pass from me.*

43

Political expediency and gallant affability,
and at times a careless gaiety,
combined with a genuine dislike
of disappointing others,
meant many left a meeting with Franklin
confident they had won the day.
Because he admired, as lawyers do,
a honed and elegant argument,
they assumed his admiration meant
assent. When his actions proved otherwise,
he appeared mercurial, deceptive.
I'd hear my voice droning on declaiming
Franklin's need to weigh the interests
of the state, then the nation, against
those of a few, regarding it my duty
to comb the sea wrack back
into political waters whenever possible.
But sometimes my view was aligned
with that of the perplexed man
or woman before me: then I'd convey
my sympathies as discreetly and clearly
as my bowed head, steady gaze,
my hands clasping theirs, my tone
could suggest—short of promise or disloyalty.

44

I was in California and could not attend Marian
Anderson's Freedom Concert performed at the foot

of the Lincoln Memorial, although I heard her,
of course, on the radio. Seventy-five thousand

Americans, the first fully integrated audience
of that size . . . I wish I'd been just another

anonymous citizen standing in the sunshine
that day, listening to the contralto Toscanini

called *the voice of a century.* Miss Anderson sang
arias and spirituals, "Nobody Knows the Trouble

I've Seen" and "America the Beautiful." Harold Ickes
spoke first and declared, *In this great auditorium*

under the sky, all of us are free . . .
Miss Anderson had sung in the White House

three years earlier, and I had the devil to pay then,
and that February, when I'd resigned

my membership in the Daughters of the American
Revolution in protest because they forbade

performances by Negro artists in their Constitution
Hall, I paid the devil again. Miss Anderson said

she was *shocked beyond words to be barred*
from the capital of my own country after having

appeared in almost every other capital of the world.
Franklin exclaimed that as far as he was concerned,

she can sing from the top of the Washington Monument
if she wants to. How deeply sad and troubling

some of the hatemongers in our own society are:
that rabid Catholic priest from Detroit,

Father Coughlin, for example, spewing the most
vile and ghastly antisemitism . . . We were giving

comfort to Hitler, Franco, and Mussolini through
our enduring racial injustice, our anti-immigrant

and isolationist policies. A month before Miss
Anderson sang before the statue of the Great

Emancipator, Hitler invaded Prague and took
over Czechoslovakia. My husband had just

recognized Franco's Spain. I yearned for the entire
idea of war to be obsolete, but now there was

renewed bloodshed everywhere. Japan had attacked
China. All free peoples of Europe, those of the Jewish

faith in particular, were in peril, or soon would be,
and here we were, with nearly two hundred

separate legislative bills introduced in Congress,
any one of which, if enacted, would have made it

a federal crime to hunt down and murder, by lynching,
a fellow citizen: each bill thwarted or withdrawn,

and then this pettiness from the DAR: it defied imagination.

45

Painful for me, at times, to be so delicately
diplomatic with those petitioners who failed

to win over Franklin and sought me out for
consolation or encouragement—as with

the anti-lynching legislation Franklin failed
to support five years going, or his refusal

to send matériel or troops to shore up
those brave souls fighting Franco in Spain.

For, on all matters, once Franklin made up
his mind, he was rarely dissuaded. And then

there were always those Southern Democrats
he had to appease with this or that. I had

only the power of access, of bringing to light
matters that otherwise would have escaped

his attention. Often, in the early hours
of the morning, after I had finished writing

the last of the day's letters, wearing my robe
and slippers, my hair in a net, I would slip

downstairs to his office to leave a note or two
on his desk, or an article—*Read this. E* clipped

to it, and he would because he knew I'd raise
the issue the next time we were at table. This

I did persistently when morally compelled—
the greatest good for the greatest number

writ into the design of my life, as into his,
public service binding us more than love

or honor, although we bickered over when
and how to achieve the ends we both desired.

His personality? Willful. Wily when need be.
Brusque at times. Deflective rather than direct.

Genial. Quick with a quip. Stubborn. Politic
even with our children and especially his mother.

46

That frightful clanging—

an alarm for a fire nearby—
and a fast burst of fear
still steals my breath,

and for years, I awoke
trembling because,
once again, I dreamt

I smelled charred flesh.
My beloved Aunt Pussie,
my mother's sister, died

when she and her two
young daughters were
smothered by smoke.

After their deaths,
I could not shake my dread
of fire, nor the sight

of their three coffins
before Holy Trinity's altar.
Of course, I was afraid

of Franklin becoming
trapped. In the White
House, his mahogany

wardrobe blocked the
passageway between
our rooms, and, quite often,

writing letters late into
the night, I heard—
over and over, for out

of his terror he practiced
this drill fanatically—
Franklin throwing his body

to the floor—THUNK!—
a sound like clay striking
the lid of a lowered coffin.

Then the slow scrape
and drag of his lifeless
legs across the floor—

drag, scrape, drag, scrape,
drag—a sound that chills
me to this day, the pure

sound of helplessness
that is in each of us,
helpless before so much

that befalls us, the sound
of Franklin's helplessness
before infantile paralysis,

before war, before a heart
slowly starved of oxygen.
One drops into the dark

trusting the floor is there
and sufficient strength
will come to crawl,

to drag the impossible weight.

47

In 1939, when the MS *St. Louis*
filled with nine hundred and thirty-
seven German refugees, desperate

human beings, sailed toward the Port
of New York, Franklin refused to
allow that ship to enter. Cordell

Hull persuaded him that it would
be impolitic to admit Semites:
the Dixiecrats again. Those poor

people—men, women, children—
were returned to Europe and many
became causalities of Hitler's

systematic extermination.
Franklin did not fully realize
what fate beheld them, none

of us did, yet great suffering
was not alleviated when he alone
was entirely capable of offering
                        safe harbor.

48

I'd cringe inwardly when I'd hear Franklin

defend himself with that jovial laugh of his
and the words *I am a practical politician*
said in that arch tone that signaled not
to press him further. So much suffering

wrought because his imagination went only
so far. Not that he didn't inspire others, or think
through the arming and mobilizing of our nation
when war finally did come, but this was

the man beloved for saying *We have nothing
to fear, but fear itself.* He could say this
in such rousing and impassioned tones
because fear, in himself, and in his children,

was plainly forbidden. Being afraid
was incompatible with being a Roosevelt.
True on my side of the family as well:
consider Uncle Teddy and his bully pulpit,

his leading the charge up San Juan Hill.
I think that perhaps my father drank,
and drank himself to death, because he
was afraid in a world where there was

no place for fear. Franklin's exuberant
confidence, his unrelenting optimism,
which I concede did do the country good,
was dissembling polished to such a high sheen—

he was himself dazzled by it.

49

April 1945

Slowly, along the eight hundred miles
of track from Warm Springs to Washington,

we carried Franklin's body home. I, alone,
in a Pullman—exhausted—yet keyed up

thinking of all I had to do in the next days.
And there, through a day and night

and into the next, at every small crossroads
or town, along the streets of cities,

or in clusters at the edge of fields,
people waited beside the tracks to pay

tribute to Franklin. Men took off hats,
held them to their chests, bowed their heads;

boys stood with arms around the shoulders
of sweetheart or sister, the women weeping,

the men weeping. Once I glimpsed four
Negroes in a cotton field fall to their knees

in prayer. "Rock of Ages" or "Abide with Me"
floated through the windows—church choirs

waiting trackside, their voices swelling
when they saw my face. Their children

wrapped in blankets, parents held them high
so one day they might remember the train

that had carried Roosevelt home. I wept at such
a tide of sorrow. At nightfall, we darkened the cars,

lit only the last, the president's, so his catafalque,
draped in our flag, could be seen for miles.

———————

I moved outside of myself then and entered

the pageant of the public mourner. Caught up
in this tempest of grief, lost, bleak, vague

in myself, I felt surprised, nonetheless,
by this great outpouring. I knew the man

in his weaknesses and shortcomings, his
failings as a father, husband, friend. He had

betrayed me yet again, so I learned within
minutes of arriving at Warm Springs, for his

cousin, Laura Delano, told me Lucy Mercer
Rutherford was with him when his cerebral

hemorrhage struck. She had dined at the White
House several times that year, their meetings

arranged and "covered" by our daughter.
Franklin had promised me, on condition I not

divorce him, he would never see her again.
That last spring, with Franklin's circle

of intimates shrunken, this loneliest of men,
reached out to me once more for companionship.

I declined his request. My awful failing
is not forgetting a hurt, rarely forgiving one.

———————

That night we carried Franklin's body back
to Washington, I drew back the window

curtain of my berth and until dawn watched
those lining the tracks. Their bodies—the very

body of the nation—seemed to pass through
my recumbent form. Then I took in the scope

of what Franklin and I had begun in those
Groton woods beside the Nashua River

when we pledged ourselves to one another
forty-two years before. Ours was the sweet

and idealized love of youth immersed in
the illusions no one in our lives dispelled

us of—I was nineteen, he, twenty-one, still
at Harvard. Oh, I took back from him years ago

my vulnerability, sealed myself like a housewife
seals her preserves with paraffin. He had his

"second wife," Missy LeHand, whose company
I never begrudged him. I had my loves, Earl,

Lorena, my life apart from his. There were five
children to live for, appearances to maintain—

our country, the Depression, war, the world's
future . . . What had become of that immense

passion? Surely it was here, in those men
and women weeping as if a saint had died

instead of a brittle, irascible, complicated man,
a man ruled by desires and whims, a need

for subterfuge, flattery, a man of such
particular thoughtlessness, in certain regards,

he could stun me to disbelief, and yet
a lonely man, desperate for companionship,

who flirted because he could not bear
solitude. All the while he had the people—

how beautiful their hands, their faces,
the reverence and dignity of their bearing.

As was not true with me, yet so with them—
in all the things that were of real, permanent

importance—he never let them down.
In the years to come, spoken in the thousands

of varied accents we Americans have,
causing my throat to clutch, my tears to rise—

hundreds upon hundreds would say to me,
Mrs. Roosevelt, I loved your husband.

———

When we buried Franklin, West Point cadets
raised their rifles and cracked the crisp air.

After each volley Fala barked, a child whimpered,
and as always happens in life, something

was coming to an end, something new beginning.
That frisky trickster, that little black fluff ball

of non-judging attention—those were his barks
whose Scottish soul, Franklin once declared,

was furious when some Republicans concocted
the story he'd been left behind on one of the Aleutians.

The president, they claimed, sent a destroyer back
to pick him up . . . at a cost to the taxpayers

of two or three, or eight or twenty million dollars—
my husband's campaign speech to the Teamsters.

I have a right to resent, to object to libelous
statements about my dog, Franklin rolled out

in his most droll tone, after having shaken his head
with chagrin: *He's not been the same dog since.*

———

I mourned Franklin genuinely and with
all the complex, contrary, and varied

emotions that marked our forty years
of marriage. I did not weep. Our wedding

day was Saint Patrick's Day, 1905, when
Uncle Teddy, then president, stepped away

from the parade he was leading through
the streets of New York, and stole all

the attention. Our marriage's last day, in 1945
fell three days short of the eightieth anniversary

of Lincoln's death, Franklin died in
the Little White House in Georgia,

not the White House, and there beside him,
Lucy Mercer Rutherford, not me. What

a glorious and tragical and ironical life
my marriage gave me. Joined by Holy Sacrament,

by our children's lives, our baby's death, through
Franklin's paralysis and his political triumphs,

but mostly by our common dream of better,
happier, more just lives for all people of goodwill;

ours was a marriage accommodated in private,
performed in public, yet we admired and respected

one another, although oftentimes, begrudgingly.

After the
White House

50

Who was I if not Franklin's
unwanted, if respected, nemesis,

his hair shirt, his harasser, waving my
moral standard, unsmiling, cheerless?

*Franklin, this action must be taken . . . This
congressman placated . . . This reform pursued.*

I could never relax, never enjoy, completely,
his bonhomie, his sparkle. Had I become

such a cynic? So disillusioned by love,
I assumed others felt as I felt? That columnist—

who was he?—O'Donnell?—who wrote—
Franklin's problem with Eleanor is she's too

ethical for him. Too ethical, too driven,
too demanding. Uncompromising.

It's almost as if it took his death—though
I hate to think it—for me to find an easy

gentleness of manner, to shuck off
the driven self's hard-driving relentlessness—

too late to be what his heart needed.

51

1946

The fate of war refugees was an issue I cared
        deeply about, not only
the pitiable Jewish survivors of the death
        camps, but other displaced
persons as well—Lithuanians, Estonians, Poles,

Ukrainians, Byelorussians, Latvians. The Yugoslav,
        and, of course, the Soviet
position, was that any refugee who refused to
        return was either a *quisling*—
collaborator—or a traitor. They proposed forcing

refugees to return to their country of origin
        and accept whatever punishment
was meted out. Most were living in flimsy, frigid,
        unsanitary camps. I felt strongly—
and most in the West agreed—they were simply

suffering people who either fled Germany in fear
        for their lives or who survived
occupation or internment against all odds.
        They ought to be free to live
wherever they felt their families might thrive,

in any country that granted them entry.
        Since V-E Day, hundreds
of thousands of children had been born.
        Would the Soviets have each
nation raise the children in state-run orphanages,

robbing the parents of their lone remaining solace?
           And, in the case of German
Jews, how could we return them to a nation
           the world had condemned
for its rapacious antisemitism? Delegates

spent endless hours attempting to frame
           a resolution all might sign.
The Soviets challenged each attempt. Vyshinsky,
           one of Russia's great
legal minds, a man expert in wielding wit and ridicule,

spoke twice. I was the only woman member
           of our delegation to the United Nations.
The men huddled behind my back, sent Dulles
           to ask, and he did so
quite lamely—*Mrs. Roosevelt, the United States*

must speak in this debate. Do you think you could
           say a few words?
Say a few words? You'd think he wanted me to
           address the garden club's
June luncheon. I debated the famous Mr. Vyshinsky.

I did my best. The hour was late. The Russians
           delayed the vote in hope some
of our allies would tire and leave. I knew I must
           hold the South Americans,
so I spoke of Simón Bolívar who had fought for

freedom from Spanish colonial control, whose
           fighters had secured independence
for a good part of Hispanic America. I became,
           at that moment, speaking before
the General Assembly, Mademoiselle Souvestre.

I saw her rolling down the map of the world
        that hung in her library,
heard her speak again of the injustice of colonial rule.
        And I saw as well, images
of the gaunt and starved survivors in their striped

rags who greeted our Allies when they liberated
        the German camps. The South
American representatives stayed and voted with us.
        We won. Of course
the United Nations would concern itself with the fate

of these refugees for many years, but the principle
        of the right of individuals
to choose where they wish to live, was secured.
        My voice trembled, my legs shook,
my hands clutched the podium. I do not know

where I find the strength at such times, only that
        it is not my doing. I wished
Franklin had heard me, and Mademoiselle Souvestre,
        and, of course, my father.
Mine was an old woman's victory, one to savor deeply,
        quietly, but it was a victory.

52

1947

Once, when I chaired the Commission
struggling to write the Universal Declaration
of Human Rights, I thought our work might

be advanced by an informal atmosphere,
so I asked a small group to meet at my
apartment for tea: a Chinese representative,

a Canadian representative, a third from Lebanon.
Chang was particularly skillful at quoting
some apt Chinese proverb to fit any occasion.

As we settled down on chairs and sofa,
and Mildred brought in tea, on a late October
afternoon, one of the three made a remark

with philosophical implications. A heated
discussion ensued. Chang, a pluralist,
argued for more than one kind of ultimate

reality. Humphrey was a realist and
a materialist. Malik expounded at length
on the philosophy of Thomas Aquinas.

Chang suggested the Secretariat spend
a few months studying the fundamentals
of Confucianism. I contented myself with

refilling their cups and sipping my tea.
The men's voices seemed to soften and move
away. I sunk back into the sofa and began

to consider human nature, my own, that
of my children and a few I had loved. I recalled
how sickened and hammered I felt the year

before, when, as a member of the US Delegation,
our plane circled above the ruins of Cologne,
Frankfort, Munich, the miles and miles of rubble

that had been Berlin. Later, touring a crowded,
decrepit Jewish refugee camp, Zeilsheim, an old
woman suddenly came upon me, knelt in

the muddy road, threw her arms around my
knees and murmured over and over *Israel! Israel!*
I still see her sunken eyes and weather-beaten

face, hear her desperate plea. And I'm weary
of still more news of lynchings and countless other
degrading acts committed against Negro citizens,

and now this new Red Scare, so reminiscent
of what went on after the First World War.
Porcelain cups clicked against saucers, the men,

my guests, uncrossed and recrossed their legs,
leaned forward or back in their chairs, hands
gestured, mouths moved. What good is

history, I wondered, if no one ever learns?

53

Hollywood made a movie about Fala, and he was
in the newsreels frequently. After the war,
wherever I traveled, people wanted to hear

about the late president's dog first, then about
the Universal Declaration of Human Rights.
Only "Master" was allowed to feed Fala.

A bone came each morning on the president's
breakfast tray, and many a visiting dignitary
cooled his heels of an evening until Fala finished

his supper, taken in the president's study.
I can still hear him speaking to that dog, his
playful, high-pitched teasing, more endearments

and flattery, more tenderness expressed than
he'd ever used with the children. Fala loved
nothing so much as taking a drive with

the president when he drove his open-topped
Phaeton, the only passenger of his never
to turn pale with fear at Franklin's rather

imprecise steering and breakneck speed.
Of course, it fell to the Secret Service to
walk him. Their code name for Fala was

the *Informer*—a little Scottie dog escorted
by a uniformed guard near a stopped train was
all someone needed to spot—and security was lost.

54

Aboard the Tuscaloosa once in the West Indies,

the sailors were cooling off on deck, stretched out in
a row, bare feet lined up. Fala caused quite a commotion

by moving quickly along the row licking and tickling.
More and more sailors removed shoes and socks

not to be bested by those already foot-licked by
the world's most famous dog. Another time,

on a fishing trip to Florida, a pile of caught fish
flip-flopping on deck, Fala lay down and began

flip-flopping too, a game he continued to play until
the day he died, with me, at Val-Kill. When I buried

him in the rose garden, beside the sundial, and at
the feet of Master, I admit my tears came in torrents.

I hadn't shed a tear at Franklin's funeral or burial,
but I wept unabashedly that day. I know my children

think I was weeping, at last, for father, but not so.
I was weeping for Fala. I was weeping for our dog.

55

Finding myself first lady of the State
    of New York; then first lady

of the United States; later a delegate
    to the United Nations General Assembly;

finding myself first chair of the UN Commission
    on Human Rights; then ambassador-at-large:

all of these positions of authority caused me to feel,
    at first, immensely uncomfortable,

inadequate, even terrified. Each time a new world
    opened at my feet and I stood on a precipice:

What could I trust in myself to carry on?
    Who said *Eleanor, you can do this?*

I knew my own heart, knew I was good, knew
    all true accomplishments are composed

of separate individual acts of courage. I trusted
    I could love, could literally generate love when needed.

I do not think I know anything else of genuine use.

56

I turn over the word horror—

horrid, horrify, horrible

I turn over the word

longing to yoke what horror is

to what horror says

but the gap is a chasm

the r three times, the o twice

the h that may connote Hell

the horror of Pearl Harbor

the horror of the Holocaust

the horror of Hiroshima

an anguished cry—

a man's or a woman's or a child's

the o, the o, the o, carried off, echoing . . .

57

When I was a young girl,
and later, a young wife
and mother, I believed that

each thing that happened
to me was significant
in some way, and quite

frequently, ironic. Now
that I am an old woman,
life is like a fog bank my

skiff passes through only
moments before another
fog bank envelops me.

Some mysteries are amusing
and lovely, some dreadfully
horrifying, but there I am,

facing whatever and whoever
emerges before me, bearing
in mind, mind you, each matter,

each person, is always more
complex and various than we
would have it, or them, be.

Epilogue

58

When I look back over my life,
at every critical juncture,
my fundamental sense of humanity
was at stake, and that is
always the issue, isn't it?

Love finds us so our empathy
toward others can grow.

Anguish finds us so compassion
grows.

The woman praised and honored—
world citizen, humanitarian,
statesman—Eleanor Roosevelt—

whoever that woman is—

she is the creation of the men
and women I loved—
they gave her to me
and I gave her away.

Notes on Poems

Epigraphs after the title page:
"When will our consciences grow so tender . . .": "My Day," February 16, 1946, and "No woman has ever . . .": Clare Boothe Luce, May 21, 1950, as cited by Allida Black in *The Eleanor Roosevelt Papers*, 2:412, 282.

Poem 17: "I was alone on my thirty-fifth birthday . . .": *Grief* was the popular name given to the bronze sculpture made by Augustus Saint-Gaudens, more accurately titled *The Mystery of the Hereafter and the Peace of God that Passeth Understanding*. It was commissioned by the historian Henry Adams as a memorial to his wife, Clover Adams. The shrouded figure is seated against a granite block, and there is hexagonal marble seating around the figure. This was ER's favorite spot for private contemplation in Washington, D.C., and a place she sometimes brought friends who were in need of consolation.

Poem 22: "Brilliant blue-sky days . . .": The quote at the end of this poem ("In back of tranquility lies always conquered unhappiness") was a sentence ER enjoyed repeating from *The Countryman's Year*, a book apparently kept at the Campobello house. It was written by David Grayson, a pen name for Ray Stannard Baker.

Poem 32: "Years later, when Lorena and I . . .": The line "I never lost a feeling of kinship for anyone who is suffering" comes from Carl Rowen's interview with ER in 1957 as quoted in his book *Dream Makers, Dream Breakers: The World of Justice Thurgood Marshal* (1993).

Poem 45: "Painful for me, at times, to be so delicately . . .": The phrase "the greatest good for the greatest number" derives from Jeremy Bentham, the English philosopher. The phrase is the common way people in the US, including Eleanor Roosevelt, came to think of Jeremy Bentham's phrase in *A Fragment on Government* "the greatest happiness of the greatest number of people."

Poem 47: "In 1939, when the MS *St. Louis* . . ." Cordell Hull was FDR's Secretary of State, serving from 1933 until 1944. While the name Dixiecrats was not the official name used by this faction of the Democratic Party until 1948 (when the States' Rights Democratic Party was formed), I am using it here to signify the conservative Democrats from the South who sometimes voted as a block in opposition to what they perceived as FDR's too liberal and progressive agenda. FDR regarded them as obstructionist and was inclined to compromise with them and avoid raising their ire whenever possible.

Notes on Sources
& a Brief Bibliography

This text is an act of literary imagination. I make no claims for its historical validity, although, of course, it is based on a real person whose life is of great historical significance. I have tried to stay true to known facts whenever possible, without hesitating to interpret Eleanor Roosevelt's subjective experience. The historic record is spotty: dairies and letters, which might have told us more, are lost or were destroyed, and Eleanor Roosevelt, although a prolific writer (who wrote countless essays, speeches, newspaper columns, and four autobiographies), shaped a rather distorted public persona. She believed in a clear separation of private life and public life, and, like the rest of us, was capable of misremembering and reinventing her own history. My inventions are particularly apparent, to me, in the case of her relationship to Earl Miller, Lorena Hickok, and David Gurewitsch. In the case of Miller, no correspondence to or from ER survives, despite thirty years of almost daily exchanges. A good portion of the Roosevelt-Hickok correspondence has disappeared or was redacted.

I have relied heavily on the work of Roosevelt's major biographer, Blanche Wiesen Cook, whose three-volume biography is the most comprehensive. Cook's work is the work of a lifetime, and I am, as all of us should be, profoundly indebted to her contribution to the historical record. There are other sources I made use of as well, in addition to the Cook biographies; most are listed below.

Asbell, Bernard, ed. *Mother and Daughter: The Letters of Anna and Eleanor Roosevelt*. New York: Viking Press, 1982.

Black, Allida, ed. *The Eleanor Roosevelt Papers: Volume 1; The Human Rights Years; 1945-1948*. Charlottesville: University of Virginia Press, 2010.

—, ed. *The Eleanor Roosevelt Papers: Volume 2; The Human Rights Years; 1949-1953*. Charlottesville: University of Virginia Press, 2012.

Cook, Blanche Wiesen. *Eleanor Roosevelt: Volume 1; 1884–1933*. New York: Viking, 1992.

—. *Eleanor Roosevelt: The Defining Years, 1933–1938*. New York: Viking, 1999.

—. *Eleanor Roosevelt: The War Years and After, 1939–1962*. New York: Viking, 2016.

Gerber, Robin. *Leadership the Eleanor Roosevelt Way: Timeless Strategies from the First Lady of Courage*. New York: Portfolio/Penguin, 2002.

Goodwin, Doris Kearns. *No Ordinary Time: Franklin and Eleanor Roosevelt; The Home Front in World War II*. New York: Simon & Schuster, 1994.

Gurewitsch, Edna P. *Kindred Souls: The Friendship of Eleanor Roosevelt and Dr. David Gurewitsch*. New York: St. Martin's Press, 2002.

Hickok, Lorena A. *Eleanor Roosevelt: Reluctant First Lady*. New York: Dodd Mead, 1962.

Lash, Joseph P. *Eleanor and Franklin: The Story of Their Relationship Based on Eleanor Roosevelt's Private Papers*. New York: W.W. Norton & Company, 1971.

Lash, Joseph P. *Eleanor: The Years Alone*. New York: William S. Konecky, 1972.

Lash, Joseph P. *A World of Love: Eleanor Roosevelt and Her Friends 1943–1962*. New York: Doubleday, 1984.

O'Farrell, Brigid. *She Was One of Us: Eleanor Roosevelt and the American Worker*. New York: Cornell UP, 2010.

Pottker, Janice. *Sara and Eleanor: The Story of Sara Delano Roosevelt and Her Daughter-in-Law, Eleanor Roosevelt*. New York: St. Martin's, 2004.

Roosevelt, Eleanor. *The Autobiography of Eleanor Roosevelt.* Cambridge, MA: Da Capo Press, 1992. (Includes *This Is My Story* [1937]; *This I Remember* [1949]; *On My Own* [1958]; and *The Search for Understanding* [1961].)

—. *Courage in a Dangerous World: The Political Writings of Eleanor Roosevelt.* Edited by Allida Mae Black. New York: Columbia University Press, 1999.

—. *My Day: The Best of Eleanor Roosevelt's Acclaimed Newspaper Columns, 1936–1962.* Edited by David Emblidge. Cambridge, MA: Da Capo Press, 2001.

—. *You Learn by Living: Eleven Keys for a More Fulfilling Life.* New York: Harper & Row, 1960.

Rosen, Robert N. *Saving the Jews: Franklin D. Roosevelt and the Holocaust.* New York: Thunder's Mouth Press, 2006.

Streitmatter, Rodger, ed. *Empty Without You: The Intimate Letters of Eleanor Roosevelt and Lorena Hickok.* New York: The Free Press, 1998.

Acknowledgments

Early versions of a few of these poems were vetted by members of The Brickwalk Poets to whom I am grateful: in particular Jim Finnegan, Clare Rossini, Ben Grossberg, Charlie Chase, and David Epstein. My thanks go to Robert Cording and Brad Davis for their comments and the nurture their friendship has given me.

A few poems from this collection, under the titles "Eleanor Discovers Lucy Mercer's Letters," "The Nomination," and "The Surprise," were published in *Drunken Boat*, Issue 12, September 2010.

I am indebted to several friends who encouraged me in this work by listening critically and generously when I read in public, particularly Richard Hoffman, Marcia McGowan, and Celia Catlett, and to those few who read the text and offered suggestions and corrections: Nan Meneely, Sharon Olson, and Baron Wormser. My heart is with these, and with those remarkable poets who have gathered at Chester each of the last eight years, especially Carole Stasiowski, Anne Harding Woodward, Lawrence Wray, and Ruth Foley (in addition to Nan and Sharon).

Midway through this project, I benefitted from a residency at the Vermont Studio Center, where a number of poems were written and others revised.

I would not have persisted in this work without Rennie McQuilkin's enthusiasm and encouragement, and that given to me by Renee Rhodes, Nancy Reuben, Rick Barrett, Charles Douthat, Julie Leff, and my husband, Bruce Gregory. I am deeply grateful to each of you.

Joan Cusack Handler's belief in the value of this work, her encouragement, and her fidelity to her authors, has mattered most of all.

CavanKerry's Mission

CavanKerry is committed to expanding the reach of poetry and other fine literature to a general readership by publishing works that explore the emotional and psychological landscapes of everyday life and relationships.

Other Books in the Notable Voices Series

Printing this book on 30-percent PCW and FSS-certified paper saved 2 trees, 1 million BTUs of energy, 127 pounds of CO_2, 67 pounds of solid waste, and 524 gallons of water.

Eleanor has been set in Garamond Premier Pro, an old-style serif typeface, named for sixteenth-century Parisian engraver Claude Garamond, which was designed by Robert Slimbach in 1988 and published by Adobe.